Journey to Freedom®

GEORGE WASHINGTON CARVER

BY CHARLES W. CAREY JR.

"IT IS NOT THE STYLE OF CLOTHES ONE WEARS, NEITHER THE KIND OF AUTOMOBILE ONE DRIVES, NOR THE AMOUNT OF MONEY ONE HAS IN THE BANK, THAT COUNTS. THESE MEAN NOTHING. IT IS SIMPLY SERVICE THAT MEASURES SUCCESS."

— GEORGE WASHINGTON CARVER

Cover and page 4 caption:
George Washington Carver
in 1925

Content Consultant:
Curtis Gregory, park ranger,
George Washington Carver
National Monument

Published in the United States of America by The Child's World®
1980 Lookout Drive, Mankato, MN 56003-1705
800-599-READ • www.childsworld.com

ACKNOWLEDGEMENTS

The Child's World®: Mary Berendes, Publishing Director

The Design Lab: Kathleen Petelinsek, Design; Gregory Lindholm, Page Production

Red Line Editorial: Holly Saari, Editorial Direction

PHOTOS

Cover and page 4: Hulton Archive/Stringer/Getty Images

Interior: Arthur Rothstein/Library of Congress, 5; George Washington Carver National
Monument, 6, 7, 9, 11, 13, 20, 21, 23; Markus Guhl/iStock Photo, 10; Iowa State University/
Special Collections Department, 14, 15, 16; Library of Congress, 17; Benjamin Frances Johnston/
Library of Congress, 19; AP Images, 22, 27; Bettmann/Corbis, 24; Ermin Gutenberger/iStock
Photo, 25

LIBRARY OF CONGRESS CATALOGING-IN-PUBLICATION DATA

Carey, Charles W.

George Washington Carver / by Charles W. Carey Jr.

p. cm.   (Journey to freedom)

Includes bibliographical references and index.

ISBN 978-1-60253-123-9 (library bound : alk. paper)

1. Carver, George Washington, 1864?–1943—Juvenile literature. 2. African American agriculturists—Biography—Juvenile literature. 3. Agriculturists—United States—Biography—Juvenile
literature. I. Title. II. Series.

S417.C3C27 2009

630.92—dc22

[B]

2009003645

CONTENTS

Chapter One

A POWERFUL SPEECH

O n May 27, 1942, college students at Selma University in Selma, Alabama, listened to George Washington Carver speak. His speech congratulated the graduating class of 1942. Selma University awarded Carver an honorary doctorate. Honorary degrees are usually given to someone who has great achievements in an area of study. Carver had been working for many years as a scientist and a teacher. He was honored for his contributions to science and **agriculture**.

At the end of his speech, Carver read aloud his favorite poem, "Equipment" by Edgar A. Guest. The closing words of the poem were powerful:

George Washington Carver was a deeply spiritual man. He credited his achievements to a higher power. Carver's faith was a main reason he spent his life in service to others.

Courage must come from the soul within,
The man must furnish the will to win.
So figure it out for yourself, my lad.
You were born with all that the great have had,
With your equipment they all began,
Get hold of yourself and say: "I can."

Carver truly believed these words. He used his knowledge and talent to develop useful products. He showed farmers in the South how to grow better crops and raise themselves out of poverty. Carver's life also proved skin color did not matter when it came to making a difference in people's lives.

George Washington Carver inspecting a crop around 1900

A statue of a young George Washington Carver is at the Carver National Monument near Diamond, Missouri.

Chapter Two

A YOUNG BOY IN MISSOURI

George Washington Carver was born on a farm near Diamond, Missouri, around 1864. At that time, slavery was legal in many U.S. territories and states, including Missouri. George's mother, Mary, was a slave. Her master was a man named Moses Carver.

Children born to slaves became the property of their parents' master. When George was born, he became a slave owned by Moses. George's older brother, Jim, was also a slave. George's father was most likely a slave on a nearby farm. He died before George was born.

Shortly after George was born, bandits kidnapped him and his mother. Moses Carver

Before slavery ended, slaves usually had only a first name. After slavery ended, many former slaves took the last names of their former masters. For example, George took the last name of his former master, Moses Carver, to become George Carver.

hired a neighbor, John Bentley, to find his slaves. He offered Bentley a horse valued at $300. Bentley supposedly found George in Arkansas. But he did not find Mary. She was never seen again.

After Mary was gone, Moses Carver still owned George and Jim as slaves. The brothers were taken in and cared for by the Carvers. In 1865, slavery was **abolished**. George and Jim were free. But Moses and his wife, Susan, continued to care for and raise the young boys.

George had health problems. He was too frail to help Moses and Jim with the farm chores. So Susan taught him other tasks. George helped with the family's cooking, cleaning, sewing, and laundry. Susan also taught him how to read from an old spelling book. George even learned to play Moses's old violin. George was an intelligent boy. He quickly mastered whatever he wanted to learn.

George also spent much of his time wandering in the woods around the Carver farm. He loved nature. He passed hours inspecting the insects and reptiles he found. Sometimes he would bring the creatures home and hide them. When Susan discovered this, she began asking George to empty his pockets before entering the house.

His favorite pastime was to gather different plants that grew in the area. He collected the seeds of the prettiest wildflowers and planted them in a secret garden. George seemed to have a natural talent for

George Washington Carver's
former master, Moses Carver

nursing plants back to health. He became known around the town of Diamond as "the plant doctor."

Soon George yearned to learn more than Susan's spelling book could teach him. But the Carvers could not instruct him further because they had little education themselves. Diamond's public school would not allow George to attend because he was black. The event was one of many experiences with **segregation** that George would face in his life.

It is believed that when George was about 11 years old, the Carvers found a **tutor** for him. After only a few months, bright, young George had learned as much as his tutor could teach him. George was certain there was much more he could learn. "I wanted to know the name of every stone and flower and insect and bird and beast," he would later recall. "I wanted to know where it got its color, where it got its life— but there was no one to tell me." With that as his motivation, George set out to investigate the world.

As a young boy, George Washington Carver loved to explore the woods by the Carver farm.

George Washington Carver around age 13 or 14

Chapter Three

SCHOOL DAYS

round 1877, when George was about 12 or 13 years old, he said goodbye to the Carvers. He moved to Neosho, Missouri, to attend a public school for black students. In Neosho, George lived with a black couple named Andrew and Mariah Watkins. He helped Mariah with the housework in exchange for room and board. After about one year, George outgrew the school in Neosho, just as he may have outgrown a tutor in Diamond. It was time to move again. This time his path led him to Kansas.

George lived in several small Kansas towns during the next few years. He attended the local public school. He also earned money to support himself by cooking, washing clothes, and doing odd jobs.

George added his middle name when he was in Kansas. He most likely added "Washington" to distinguish himself from another George Carver.

George was a talented painter, and he continued to paint throughout his life. Two of his paintings were even shown at the 1893 World's Fair in Chicago.

In the mid-1800s, George attended high school in Minneapolis, Kansas. He wanted to attend college too. So he applied to a small school in Highland, Kansas. Highland College was impressed by his grades and accepted him by mail. When George arrived for the first day of classes, however, school officials would not allow him to attend. They turned George away because he was black.

George felt discouraged. He almost gave up his dream of attending college. After he was turned away from Highland, George farmed land in western Kansas. He grew wheat and lived by himself. He earned the respect and friendship of many settlers in the area. Later, he moved to Iowa and did small jobs wherever he briefly settled.

In 1890, George decided it was time to overcome the disappointment of being barred from Highland College. He applied to Simpson College in Iowa. The school accepted him as a student. When he showed up for classes, George was not turned away.

George took many classes at Simpson College. These included grammar, arithmetic, art, essay writing, voice, and piano. He focused his studies on painting and piano.

Although George was studying the arts at school, he was still very interested in plants. He often brought in some of the plants he had grown for his art teacher, Miss Etta Budd, to admire. His knowledge of plants impressed her. She suggested he transfer to Iowa State

George Washington Carver
was a skilled painter.

College of Agriculture and Mechanic Arts (now Iowa State University). Ms. Budd's father worked there as a professor of horticulture, which is the study of plants.

George began attending Iowa State in 1891. There he changed his focus of study from the arts to the sciences. George learned a lot about plants. It was not long before George became one of the best students

George Washington Carver in Iowa State's military **regiment** clothes in 1894

George Washington Carver's 1894 graduation photo from Iowa State

at Iowa State. He learned to breed two plants from different species to make a **hybrid**. Scientists create hybrids to be stronger or prettier, or to bear better-tasting fruits and vegetables than the parent plants.

George was involved in many activities at Iowa State. These included the debate club, the Young Men's Christian Association (YMCA), and the school's military regiment. He also wrote poetry and worked in the school's dining hall.

George received a **bachelor's degree** in 1894. He decided to stay at Iowa State a while longer because leaders in the horticulture department asked him to teach classes. George became the college's first black **faculty** member. He managed the school's greenhouse. He also studied for an advanced degree in plant science. In 1896, he received a **master's degree** in agriculture. George was the first black student to receive both a bachelor's and a master's degree from the college.

A portrait of George Washington Carver after he graduated from Iowa State

George Washington
Carver around 1906

Chapter Four

A NEW CAREER

fter his graduation in 1896, George
Washington Carver received offers
to teach at several colleges. One offer
was from Booker T. Washington, the
head of Tuskegee Institute in Alabama. Tuskegee
was a college for black students founded by
Washington in 1881. The school mainly taught
vocational skills that would help young black men
and women find jobs after graduation.

The Civil War had ended less than 20 years
earlier. Blacks were no longer slaves, but they had
a hard time finding good jobs. This was very true
in the South, where blacks were often victims of
racism and **discrimination**. Whites did not want
to work side-by-side with blacks. Whites did not

Booker T. Washington is an important figure in black history. He was a leader in black education through Tuskegee Institute and served as a spokesperson for the black community. In his "Atlanta Compromise" speech, Washington promoted vocational education for blacks. He believed this was a way of improving race relations in the South.

want blacks to take jobs that whites could have. Blacks struggled to find means to support themselves.

One way blacks earned their living was by farming. Many students at Tuskegee Institute studied farming skills. Washington wanted Carver to teach students everything he knew about agriculture. Although Washington could not offer Carver a large salary, Carver accepted the position. Like Washington, Carver wanted to help blacks improve their lives.

In 1896, Carver became the head of Tuskegee's agriculture department. He had moved around a great deal in his early life to reach his goals. After he arrived at Tuskegee, Carver never moved again.

Tuskegee did not have enough money to hire all the employees it needed. All the teachers had to pitch in and do extra jobs in addition to their teaching duties. Carver directed an experiment station where the workers tried to grow hybrids. He also managed the school's farm. Carver bought school supplies at the lowest prices. He kept the school grounds neat and green. He also attended meetings with other faculty members.

Carver did not fully enjoy these extra jobs. He did not like to tell people what to do. He felt that attending faculty meetings was often a waste of time. Perhaps his biggest problem at Tuskegee was that the school did not give him enough money to buy supplies. When Carver arrived at Tuskegee, there was no science laboratory. He had to find or make the equipment for it.

George Washington Carver (front row, center) with Tuskegee Institute faculty members around 1902

Carver had so many duties, he could not always do his extra jobs as well as he would have liked. They also took time away from Carver's mission at the school. What Carver really wanted was to spend his time experimenting with plants and teaching others what he knew. He excelled at these tasks.

At Tuskegee, Carver developed a teaching style that was different than what he used at Iowa State. Carver did not lecture his students in a formal way. Rather, he talked with them as if they were having a friendly conversation. He explained that the subjects he taught, including agriculture and chemistry, were related to each other. Sometimes, he explained things by telling jokes. Other times, he related the lesson to a story from the Bible, which many students knew well.

George Washington Carver (second from right) instructing a group of Tuskegee students

Carver taught his students by letting them discover things for themselves. He sent them out into the woods that surrounded the institute to search for plants and insects. It was similar to what he had done when he was a child. He encouraged students to conduct their own experiments. He gave them helpful suggestions when they

George Washington Carver teaching a group of students at Tuskegee Institute

made mistakes. Carver inspired his students by teaching them to appreciate the miracles and the beauty of nature. He was a popular teacher at Tuskegee.

Although he joked that he would punish his students if they did not do better in school, Carver always showed his students respect. He taught them to treat themselves and others the same way. Carver was an important influence in the lives of his students, most of whom never forgot him.

Long after they left Tuskegee, many of his former students continued to write letters to Carver. Many named their firstborn sons after him. Carver always wrote back as soon as he could. He also remembered these "grandchildren" on their birthdays and graduations.

Carver's students are not the only ones who recognized his accomplishments. In 1939, Carver was awarded the Roosevelt Medal for Outstanding Contribution to Southern Agriculture. After his death, Carver was honored on postage stamps in both 1948 and 1998.

21

George Washington Carver in his Tuskegee lab performing experiments

Chapter Five

A LIFE OF SCIENCE

In addition to teaching, Carver conducted many laboratory experiments at Tuskegee. His goal was to teach farming methods that would make life easier for poor, southern farmers. He also wanted to develop new, helpful uses for plants.

At the time Carver arrived at Tuskegee, most southern farmers only grew cotton. Growers could usually sell cotton for enough money to buy everything they needed, including tools for their farms and food for their families. George developed a better species of cotton plant. It became known as Carver's Hybrid. This new breed of cotton matured quickly. Farmers could pick the cotton before insects had a chance to destroy it.

However, Carver's Hybrid did not solve one major problem of southern farming. Farmers planted more cotton than the land could support. All plants need to absorb **nutrients** from the soil to help them grow. Cotton crops take out many important nutrients from the soil. The only way to grow cotton in the same fields every year was to use **fertilizer** that adds nutrients to the soil. Most black farmers had just enough money to rent land, buy farm tools, and feed their families. They could not afford to buy fertilizer. Without nutrients in the soil, farmers were forced to grow less cotton each year. Soon, they barely made enough money to survive.

George Washington Carver studying a plant at Tuskegee

Carver tried to help these farmers by finding ways to enrich the soil without using expensive fertilizer. He knew that **legume** plants returned nutrients to the soil. These plants acted as natural fertilizers. Carver began encouraging farmers to practice a method of planting called crop rotation. Farmers would alternate crops every other year to enrich the soil.

George Washington Carver
in a Tuskegee greenhouse
around 1940

*Carver developed more
than 100 products from
sweet potatoes. These
include:*

After-dinner mints
Chocolate
Instant coffee
Lemon drops
Library paste
Medicine
Paints
Paper (from vines)
Rubber compound
Shoe blacking
Synthetic cotton
Synthetic silk
Vinegar
Writing ink
Yeast

Carver taught farmers to alternate crops of **cowpeas** with cotton crops. This improved the quality of the soil without spending money on fertilizer. It also gave the farmers something inexpensive and nutritious to feed their families or to sell.

Carver experimented with other ways to help farmers grow inexpensive food. He developed a method to grow large sweet potato crops on small pieces of land. Then he showed farmers how to make basic foods, such as flour, sugar, and bread, from sweet potatoes. Carver also showed farmers how they could afford to eat more meat by feeding their hogs acorns instead of expensive cornmeal. Acorns were plentiful in southern forests, and people could harvest them for free.

Carver introduced soybeans and alfalfa to southern farmers. These were two crops they usually did not grow. Farmers could sell both products to factories that made paint and animal feed to make money. Carver is considered the father of chemurgy, which is the science of finding industrial uses for plant products.

Carver is most famous for introducing the peanut to southern farmers. However, he was not the first to suggest that peanuts could be an important crop. Others had suggested that people could use peanuts for a variety of things. It was Carver, though, who put these ideas and developments to good use.

Although peanuts had been grown throughout the South in the past, they were mostly used to feed livestock. Carver proved that peanuts, like other legumes, could enrich the soil. Peanuts could also provide farmers, their families, and the marketplace with an inexpensive source of **protein**. As farmers started growing more peanuts, supplies of the crop became too large. Carver set out to find new uses for peanuts.

Peanuts contain plenty of vegetable oil that can be used to make many other things. Carver developed more than 300 uses for peanuts. They included cheese, facial powder, shampoo, and printer's ink. He taught people to make items such as vinegar, a coffee-like drink, soap, medicine, and wood stain from peanuts.

Because of George Washington Carver's developments, southern farmers learned many uses for peanuts.

Carver developed more than 300 products from peanuts. Some of them include:
Caramel
Cocoa
Face powder
Gasoline
Glue
Hand cleanser
Hand lotion
Laundry soap
Mayonnaise
Pancake flour
Rubber
Shaving cream

Carver continued his research and taught at Tuskegee Institute for 47 years. He labored not for fame or fortune, but to quench his thirst for knowledge—and to help the black community.

Carver died on January 5, 1943. He left his life savings to Tuskegee to establish a museum and a research institute for agricultural chemistry at the school. The George Washington Carver Foundation is still in existence today.

During and after his life, Carver received many awards and honors. In 1923, the National Association for the Advancement of Colored People (NAACP) awarded Carver with the Spingarn Medal. This award honors great achievements by the black community. In 1939, Carver received the Roosevelt Medal for Outstanding Contributions to Southern Agriculture. In 1948, the U.S. Postal Service issued the first George Washington Carver stamp.

In July of 1943, the U.S. government declared Carver's birthplace in Diamond, Missouri, a national monument. The park stretches across 240 acres (97 ha) of what was once Moses Carver's farm. Thousands of people travel to the site each year. A museum includes exhibits about George Washington Carver's life and his many important developments. Beyond the museum, a short trail winds through the Missouri woodland and prairie. The path weaves through the landscape that helped inspire Carver to become a scientist.

George Washington Carver standing by his lab equipment in 1940

Carver's teaching and developments helped farmers to grow better crops. His contributions helped black and white southerners overcome the poverty that plagued the South during his lifetime.

Carver was buried at Tuskegee Institute. The words on his gravestone read, "He could have added fortune to fame, but caring for neither, he found happiness and honor in being helpful to the world."

Time Line

CA. 1864
George is born into slavery near Diamond, Missouri.

1865
The U.S. Civil War ends, and enslaved blacks are freed.

CA. 1877
George moves to Neosho, Missouri, to attend a school for blacks students.

1878
George moves to Kansas to attend another school.

1884 OR 1885
George attends high school in Minneapolis, Kansas.

1884 OR 1885
Highland College refuses to allow George to attend because he is black.

1890
Carver becomes a student at Simpson College in Iowa.

1891
Carver becomes the first black to attend Iowa State College of Agriculture and Mechanic Arts.

1894
Carver receives a bachelor's degree from Iowa State College of Agriculture and Mechanic Arts.

1896
Carver receives a master's degree from Iowa State College of Agriculture and Mechanic Arts.

1896
Carver begins teaching at Tuskegee Institute in Tuskegee, Alabama.

1897
Carver begins his experiments with sweet potatoes.

1903
Carver begins his experiments with peanuts.

1904
Carver begins his experiments with cowpeas.

1923
Carver receives the Spingarn Medal for his outstanding achievement in the field of science.

1939
Carver receives the Roosevelt Medal for Outstanding Contributions to Southern Agriculture.

1943
Carver dies in Tuskegee, Alabama, on January 5.

1943
The George Washington Carver National Monument is established in July.

1948
The first George Washington Carver stamp is issued.

Glossary

abolished
*(uh-**bol**-ishd)*
If something has been abolished, it has ended officially. The United States abolished slavery with the Thirteenth Amendment.

agriculture
*(**ag**-ruh-kul-chur)*
Agriculture describes tasks related to farming. Carver was a scientist in the field of agriculture.

bachelor's degree
*(**bach**-uh-lurs di-**gree**)*
A bachelor's degree is an educational degree that comes after a high school diploma. Carver earned a bachelor's degree from Iowa State College of Agriculture and Mechanic Arts.

cowpeas
*(**cow**-pees)*
Cowpeas are a type of legume. Carver used cowpeas in crop rotation.

discrimination
*(diss-krim-i-**nay**-shun)*
Discrimination is unfair treatment of people based on differences of race, gender, religion, or culture. During Carver's lifetime, blacks faced discrimination in the South.

faculty
*(**fak**-ul-tee)*
A faculty is a group of teachers. Carver was a member of the faculty at Tuskegee Institute.

fertilizer
*(**fur**-tuh-ly-zer)*
Fertilizer is a substance used on crops to make them grow better. Southern farmers used crop rotation in place of fertilizer.

hybrid
*(**hy**-brid)*
A hybrid is a plant that is bred from two different varieties of species. Carver developed a hybrid of the cotton plant.

legume
*(**le**-gyoom)*
A legume is a plant whose seeds grow in pods, such as peas, beans, and lentils. A legume that Carver worked with was the peanut.

master's degree
*(**mass**-turs di-**gree**)*
A master's degree is the educational degree that comes after a bachelor's degree. Carver earned a master's degree in agriculture from Iowa State College of Agriculture and Mechanic Arts.

nutrients
*(**noo**-tree-unts)*
Nutrients are minerals, proteins, and vitamins. Carver introduced crop rotation in order to place nutrients back into the soil.

protein
*(**proh**-teen)*
A protein is a nutrient and an essential building block of cells. Peanuts are a good source of protein.

racism
*(**ray**-sih-zum)*
Racism is the belief that one race is superior to another. During Carver's life, blacks in the South experienced racism.

regiment
*(**rej**-uh-munt)*
A regiment is a military unit. Carver was in a regiment at Iowa State.

segregation
*(seg-ruh-**gay**-shun)*
Segregation is the act of keeping members of a race, class, or ethnic group apart. Carver could not attend Highland College because of its segregation rule.

tutor
*(**too**-tur)*
A tutor is a person who gives individual lessons to a student. Carver may have had a tutor while growing up in Diamond, Missouri.

vocational skills
*(voh-**kay**-shun-ul **skilz**)*
Vocational skills are skills that an individual can use at work. Students at Tuskegee Institute developed vocational skills.

FURTHER INFORMATION

Books

Bolden, Tonya. *Portraits of African-American Heroes*. New York: Penguin, 2005.

Hudson, Wade. *Book of Black Heroes: Scientists, Healers, and Inventors*. East Orange, NJ: Just Us Books, 2002.

Laird, Roland. *Still I Rise: A Graphic History of African Americans*. New York: Sterling, 2009.

Nelson, Marilyn. *Carver: A Life in Poems*. New York: Hachette, 1997.

Troy, Don. *Booker T. Washington*. Mankato, MN: Child's World, 2009.

Videos

The Boyhood of George Washington Carver. Phoenix Learning Group, 2008.

Modern Marvels: George Washington Carver Tech. History Channel, 2005.

Web Sites

Visit our Web page for links about George Washington Carver:

http://www.childsworld.com/links

NOTE TO PARENTS, TEACHERS, AND LIBRARIANS: We routinely verify our Web links to make sure they are safe, active sites—so encourage your readers to check them out!

Index